Secrets From
My Grandma's
Garden

Published by Eversoll Enterprises, Inc., 813 Biscay Lane, Fort Collins, CO 80525

Our Mission: *To entertain, educate, and inspire through publications relating to gardening, cooking, and wood crafting.*

Manufactured in the United States of America. Printed by Vision Graphics, Loveland, CO 80538

Library of Congress Cataloging-in-publication Data

ISBN: 978-06154402-7-9

First edition

Acknowledgments: **Green Fire Times**, for permission to reprint article by Michael Martin Meléndrez, "The Story of the Aboretum Tomé", Los Lunas, NM.
Jason Gogela, cover art, graphics, and technical support.
Melissa Freier, graphic arts, layout, and technical support.
Dick Dunn, Simon Pinneger for content review and comment.
Therese Eversoll, proofreading, photographic assistance.
Children's Garden at Spring Creek for consent to photograph.
Christine Forseth, Annie Forseth, Alex Forseth, Jakob, Michael, and Katie Hobert as valuable garden helpers.

We welcome comments and communication. Please send to:
Eversoll Enterprises, 813 Biscay Lane, Fort Collins, CO 80525.

Introduction

I remember the first time I followed Grandma to her sprawling country garden, as she hobbled along the shady, cool path at the edge of the woods. It wasn't a long walk for an eight-year-old kid, but the excitement was building with every short step at what lie ahead. I had ripe strawberries on my mind.

It had rained hard the night before, and wispy little fingers of fog played hide-and-seek in the apple orchard just coming into view. These ventures down the garden path were more than just a walk to the garden. They were a trip into the heart and soul of a loving, gentle woman who cared deeply about teaching her grandkids a little something about how to grow your own food.

A few more steps and we were there. The sweet smell of ripe cantaloupe, the luscious strawberries, harvest apples and pears heralded our arrival, and giant watermelons grew in the rich, black sandy loam of the central Nebraska prairie.

Thus began for me what has become a life-long passion for growing vegetables and flowers, and also trying to understand the many nuances of their amazing lifestyles. That old farm of Grandpa and Grandma Eversoll's was long ago claimed back by Mother Nature as her own, but the overgrown bushes and twisted trees are no hindrance to my memory. All I have to do is shut my eyes, and half a century or more just melts away.

My little book is a celebration. It is meant to be instructive, to be certain. But I like what Thomas Jefferson once said: *"No occupation or pursuit is so delightful to me as the culture of the earth. And no culture comparable to that of the garden. But an old man, I am but a young gardener."*

Gardening, indeed, is a spiritual exercise for me, and no doubt for thousands of others, and I have written the following testimony to that power. It hangs over my garden gate:

KNOW ALL WHO ENTER HERE:

This garden is a sanctuary for the soul, a living wellspring of faith, hope, and promise.

The bounty and beauty of the good Earth belong to The Creator, and all who come here are witness to his Grace and Everlasting Love!!

--ENJOY !!   -PAPA DON.

To my sweet Grandmother,

Ethel Stull Eversoll,

I dedicate

this book.

Her spirit

lives deep within me.

-- Don Eversoll

The best things

are nearest: breath

in your nostrils, light

in your eyes, flowers

at your feet, duties

at your hand, the path

of God before you.

.....Robert Louis Stevenson

About the Author

Don Eversoll is an entrepreneur by trade, and gardener by heart. Born and raised in central Nebraska, he graduated from the University of Nebraska, and later became Tourism Director for the State of Nebraska, and Associate Editor of NEBRASKAland magazine. He launched BEAUTY BEYOND BELIEF, a wildflower seed company in 1989, and later BOUNTY BEYOND BELIEF, an heirloom vegetable seed firm,  with Michael Wade of Boulder, CO. Don sold both companies to Mike in 2007. Mr. Eversoll lives on a small acreage in Fort Collins with his wife, Terri, and the couple have three adult children, all whom are avid gardeners.

Don has lectured extensively on wildflowers and heirloom vegetables for more than 20 years.

*Company names used with permission of Michael Wade, Owner of BBBseed.

When Did We Get The Last Frost In The Spring?

_____

_____

_____

What Date Was The First Frost In The Fall?

_____

_____

_____

A Sense Of Stewardship

The writing of this book has evoked precious memories for me of good times past. I have strived to weave into the fabric of the book what I inherited from my ancestors: A sense of stewardship and responsibility for the environment and precious resources uniquely ours in this wonderful land we call the good 'ole USA.

It is my humble goal to empower you, the reader, with age-old wisdom yet down-to-earth advice. How fortunate it is for me to have grown up receiving both from my dear parents and grandparents on both sides of my family.

"The mind is a garden,
Your thoughts are the seeds,
The harvest can be either flowers or weeds."
--Author Unknown

"Gardeners are no less impressed by the opening of a springtime bud, than the discovery of a new star in the solar system."
--DVEversoll

List Of Things To Do:

_____

_____

_____

_____

_____

_____

_____

_____

_____

_____

A Note To The Reader

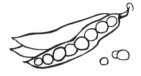

Following harvest of your vegetables, the next logical step is to get them into the kitchen where you can wash them and eat them, either out-of-hand, or cooking them alone, or even incorporating them into a delicious recipe.

In Chapter 11 you will find six favorite recipes of Grandma's that will have you licking your chops as you hustle to the stove to whip one up in time for dinner.

One important tip from Grannie: If you boil any veggies prior to eating, be sure to save the water you cooked them in. That's where some of the most important and healthy vitamins and minerals have been released. Save this liquid to make delicious soups or sauces in the future.

P.S.-- Look for Don Eversoll's second book in this series, "*Secrets from Grandma's Kitchen*" which will be released in Spring, 2011. It's a cookbook featuring over 100 mouth-watering recipes gleaned from the dog-earned and fruit-stained pages of Grannie's private family collection.

Table of Contents

Results: Soil Test Of My Garden

Date....................

_____

_____

_____

_____

_____

_____

_____

_____

_____

_____

_____

Chapter 1

How to Build Good Soil

Perhaps out of pure

heavenly goodness

the Spring came and

crowded everything it

possibly could into

that one place!

................Burnett

Building Good
Garden Soil
From Poor Dirt
Or Clay

We're going to start you off with one of the neatest little tricks of Grandma's time to get you headed down the garden path on the right foot.

In order to build good soil, you need first of all to determine the physical makeup, or composition, of the soil you wish to improve. All you need for this is a quart jar, $1^{1/2}$ cups of water, and a small trowel. Put the water in the jar, and dig up enough dirt from different areas of your garden to fill the jar to the 3/4 mark. Put a tight lid on the jar, and shake it up. Then set it aside for two days.

As you can see from the photo on the next page, the soil will separate into layers. On the very bottom will be light gravel, and the next one is sand. The next layer up is clay, and the one above that is light organic matter. At the very top will be the water.

Strive For A Balance

What you need to have good balance in your soil is an equal amount of all four components (disregard the water). This will provide good percolation and drainage, adequate retention of moisture, and some of the required nutrients. While you're at it, you might drop a ph soil tester into the jar (drain the water first), and see if it reads close to 6.5-7.5. If it's on the low side of 6.5, your soil is too acidic. If it's above 7.5, it's too alkaline.

17

The secret's in the jar. Analyzing soil composition the easy way. Note the different layers when they settle. The water is on top.

To correct the acidic condition, add agricultural lime according to the directions on the package. If too alkaline, add an acidic amendment (see your favorite nursery for a good product) and follow the directions to apply.

If you don't have a compost bin, or something similar, now is the time to start one. A wide range of bins are available from retail stores, and are preferable to one you can make yourself. Even at that, I have found that a box made from construction scrap wood performs almost as well as the commercial types (see photo). You will need to put a little more 'elbow grease' into keeping the contents turned over every once in a while, but given a little heat, your little pile of organic matter will eventually turn into a magic potion of humus and natural fertilizer.

Add Kitchen Scraps To Pile

Almost without exception, most gardens I have seen need more organic matter (humus), and the best place to start collecting the raw ingredients to make it, believe it or not, is RIGHT UNDER YOUR KITCHEN SINK. Yep, that's right. In addition to your regular trash basket you keep under the sink, just slip another one next to it, and label it 'For Compost' (See photo). Once to twice a week, take the contents out to your compost pile, or bin, and you'll be surprised how quickly it adds up. Just make sure you don't put any meat scraps into it, sticking instead of vegetables and fruit trimmings, coffee grounds, tea bags, etc.

In addition to your kitchen collection of scraps, you will need to mix in some dry grass clippings, dead leaves, and a hefty amount of dried dairy manure. I get my 'cow cookies' from a local dairy farm who trades me a couple of 5-gallon buckets of the stuff for a jar or two of home-made pickles or tomato salsa. Grandma used

Your homemade compost pile doesn't need to be fancy to be effective; this one was constructed with scrap construction plywood.

Making compost begins right under your nose (under the kitchen sink, that is). Throwing vegetable scraps in the basket is a start.

to make what she called dairy cow tea by mixing animal chips with water and applying about once a month.

Nature's Own Is Amazing!

Either way, wet or dry, you will be astonished at the results you get from using nature's own soil amendment and fertilizer. And if you decide to fashion your own compost pile from scrap wood, don't make it any deeper than 14-16 inches deep. and five by five feet wide. When finished and you have started to drop in the already-mentioned organic items, as the season progresses, throw in all the green tops you have cut from mature vegetables, like beets, kohlrabi, radish, and turnips (if you don't eat them yourself). This recycles many of the nutrients present in the tops and will help to create humic acid, the most important plant elixir to come out of any compost pile or bin.

Also try to keep a 50/50 balance in your compost pile between brown material and green matter. This means keeping a ready supply of dried grass clippings and dry leaves through the summer. Make sure you don't use grass clippings from the lawn if you have used any weed killers or insecticides. These chemicals will make their way into the soil and possibly contaminate the vegetables growing in it.

MORE ON HUMIC ACID-- As you continue to add more and more organic material to your compost pile, this is an ideal time to enrich it with more humic acid. What exactly is humic acid? It's the saviour of your soil, that's all!! Humic acid is formed when the raw ingredients of your compost pile are broken down into basic building blocks. The reason you add some humic acid to your compost is that your heap will produce a lot of humus, but probably not enough of humic acid.

Humic acid is famous for conditioning the soil, improving water holding capacity, elevating microbial activity, aiding nutrient uptake, and in short, encouraging healthy plant growth. Some say the brown liquid coming out of the bottom of a well-aged compost heap is rich in humic acid.

But to jump-start this process, you can purchase humic acid from reputable nurseries and apply at the recommended rate. You might have to wait a big longer than usual for the humic acid to work on the humus, but over several season, you will be rewarded with astonishing results. Another bonus is that over time you can eliminate the use of commercial fertilizers altogether.

Just What Is Humic Acid?

For an easy-to-understand lesson on humic acid, listen to Michael Martin Meléndrez, curator of the Albuquerque Tomé, a botanical garden near Las Lunas, New Mexico: (reprinted with permission of **Green Fire Times**):

"The science of soil and the way plants take in water and nutrients is all contingent upon a healthy 'soil food web,' a cycle of life and nutrients taking place that results in a gradual development of topsoil, what is called pedogenesis, the Creation of Soil. The very essence of rich dark topsoil is the presence and concentration of a biologic material we commonly call humus. In science the word for humus is humic substance, and within this substance is an essential product of soil chemistry called humic acid. The word substance is from the latin *substantia*, which is the real physical matter of which a person or thing consists. For example, humic acid is the substance of humus.

Humic Acids Are Long-Lasting

"For purposes of distinction, we must understand that a soil can contain organic matter and it can also contain

If only Grandma could see these new motor-driven rototillers now. The soil should be turned & churned in late fall and again in Spring.

humus. In order to know how to make dirt into a healthy soil, you must understand that humus and organic matter are not the same, and it is humic acids that are essential for a healthy and productive soil. It is also the humic acids that give us a long lasting benefit, because unlike organic matter, which decomposes rapidly turning back into CO_2, humic acids have a resonance time in the soil that can last for thousands of years.

"Nothing else in nature can bioremediate a soil as fast or as well as humic acid, and it's the black carbon-rich molecules of humic acids that, when concentrated, give a topsoil its appearance along with its chemical, physical and biological characteristics.

"In a Journal of Chemical Education (Dec. 2001) article titled *Humic Acids: Marvellous Products of Soil Chemistry*, it is stated that "Humic acids are remarkable brown to black products of soil chemistry that are essential for healthy and productive soils. They are functionalized molecules that can act as photosensitizer, retain water, bind to clays, act as plant growth stimulants, and scavenge toxic pollutants. No synthetic material can match humic acid's physical and chemical versatility."

Rich, black dirt--the result of a good compost heap or bin!

Chapter 2

Planning
Your
Garden

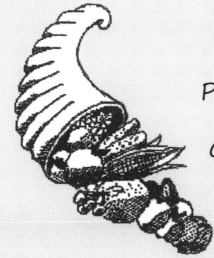

My Favorites From Last Year:

_____

_____

_____

_____

_____

_____

_____

_____

_____

_____

_____

Planning Your Garden

So, the snow is blowing outside, you're drooling over the seed catalogue on the table with all its magic and allure, and you can't wait to plant your garden. Aren't you forgetting something? Oh yes, the part about planning first.

Why plan? There are several good reasons of course, but chief among them all is a concept known as 'companion planting.' This little trick has been used for many, many years, and quite possibly was taught to the pioneers and settlers by our native American Indian tribes. Some say it was already being practiced in Europe prior to colonization. Regardless, folks in my Grandmother's era definitely knew what was going on here.

Beneficial Relationships Exist

What exactly is companion planning? Here's what it means: There is a certain beneficial relationship between some plants that when planted next to each other in the garden, produce better than when planted elsewhere. Tomatoes love carrots, for example, for some known or unknown reason and both will bear more heavily when grown in adjacent rows. Many of our outstanding universities and corporations are currently studying this phenomenon to better understand how these 'best buddy' relationships work.

What is known is that this practice can make a big difference in your garden between producing just an average crop, and a better crop. Just how close to each other are companion plants? This might seem like a quantum leap in faith for you to believe, but this is the answer: For finer leafed vegetables, plant several different ones IN THE SAME ROW, alternating between sowing lettuce for two feet, then sowing two feet of carrot, then another two feet of radish, etc, etc. Be sure to check the chart that follows for the right fit for each variety.

For other varieties, planting in adjacent rows should be sufficient. This means that you could plant onions, for example, in the row next to the tomatoes.

Concept Is Catching On

This concept at first might seem like a stretch and many folks have not practiced it up until now. But the idea is beginning to catch on and as time goes by with more and more gardeners, seed companies, university scientists, and food producers exploring the mysteries of companion plants, the magical qualities locked up in plant synergies will come to light, and thus serve to benefit the general public.

Many Native American tribes knew which plants were the best companions to grow near certain others. These early Indians were the unheralded true botanists and gardeners long before university extension departments were even a dream in the minds of pioneers and settlers.

My own Grandmother Eversoll, as a matter of pride, was 1/16 Iroquois Indian and carried that same intuition and understanding of the natural world as her ancestors. The 'companion plant' chart follows on the next page.

HERE'S A CHART TO FOLLOW IN PLANNING YOUR PLOT

Vegetable	It will like	Dislike
Beans	Carrots, peppers, cabbage family, potatoes, beets, cucumbers	Onion, garlic
Beets	Onions, kohlrabi, radishes	Climbing beans
Broccoli	All aromatic herbs, beets, onions, potatoes, brussels sprouts	- -
Brussels Sprouts	Broccoli, dill	- -
Cabbage (Includes Cauliflower)	Potatoes, onions, garlic, dill, beets, kohlrabi, turnips	Tomatoes, bean
Carrots	Lettuce, garlic, onions, peas, tomatoes, chives	- -
Celery	Cabbage, tomatoes, beans	- -
Corn	Pumpkin, squash, cucumbers	- -
Cucumbers	Corn, beans, radish, peas	- -
Eggplant	Beans	- -
Kohlrabi	Beets, beans, peas, potatoes	- -
Lettuce	Radish, cucumbers, carrots	- -
Melons	Corn	Potatoes
Onions, Garlic	Beets, tomatoes, lettuce	Beans, peas
Peas	Carrots, beans, turnips, kohlrabi, beets, radish	Potatoes
Potatoes	Corn, beans, cabbages	Squash, tomatoes, pumpkins
Pumpkins	Corn	Potatoes
Radish	Lettuce, peas, cucumbers	- -
Spinach	Peas, lettuce	- -
Squash	Corn	- -
Strawberries	Beans, lettuce	Cabbages
Tomatoes	Carrots, onions, garlic	Potatoes, cabbages, dill
Turnips	Peas, kohlrabi, beets	- -

Note: There are other companion plants for some of the varieties mentioned, but are omitted for practical purposes. Would you really want to plan bush beans or peas in your corn patch? Probably not, for the reason that the corn would tend to shade out the shorter varieties as it grows taller and taller during the season.

That good ole' kitchen table is a great place to plan your garden.

Corn should always be planted in tight clusters rather than in long rows. This insures each ear will be pollinated.

Another tip from Granny: Be sure to rotate your garden every year. Some soil-borne disease organisms tend to persist in the soil for a long period of time, and these organisms can attack vegetables from the same botanic families. For example, do not plant tomatoes where potatoes grew last year, or the year before, as they are both related (nightshade family), and they could be susceptible to the disease organisms mentioned above. In addition, if you grow one type of vegetable from the same family in one particular area for a long period of time, soil fertility might decline, and certain pests would tend to attack the plants from last year.

"In order to come up with a good crop rotation program," says Maurice Ogutu of the University of Illinois, "it is important to know different botanical families of vegetables." Ogutu lists some of these below:

Solanacea or Nightshade Family -- tomato, pepper, eggplant, potato, tomatillo

Onion Family -- onions, garlic, leek, shallot, chives

Cucurbit or Gourd Family -- cucumbers, muskmelon, watermelon, squash, pumpkin, gourd

Mustard or Cole Family -- cabbage, broccoli, cauliflower, brussels sprouts, kohlrabi, turnip, radish, chinese cabbage, kale, collards, mustard greens, rutabaga

Legume or Pea Family -- garden pea, snap beans, lima beans, soybean

Grass Family (edible part is seed) -- sweet corn, popcorn, ornamental corn

Carrot Family (edible parts are roots, leaves, and leafstalk) -- carrots, parsnip, parsley, celery

Goosefoot Family -- beet, swiss chard, spinach

Sunflower Family -- lettuce, Jerusalem artichoke, endive, salsify

Bindweed Family (edible part is root) -- sweet potato

Mallow Family (edible part is fruit) -- okra

Eye Candy--A well-designed plot is a source of great pride and promise. Most gardeners place their rows north-to-south.

A good plan calls for placing carrots, onions and tomatoes together.

The Package of Seed

I paid a dime for a package of seeds
And the clerk tossed them out with a flip;
"We've got'em assorted for every man's needs,"
He said with a smile on his lip;
"Pansies and poppies and asters and peas!
Ten cents a package! And pick as you please!"

Now seeds are just dimes to the man in the store,
And the dimes are the things that he needs;
And I've been to buy them in season before,
But have thought of them merely as seeds;
But it flashed through my mind as I took them this time,
"You have purchased a miracle here for a dime."

You've a dime's worth of power which no man can create,
You've a dime's worth of life in your hand!
You've a dime's worth of mystery, destiny, fate,
Which the wisest cannot understand.
In this bright little package, now isn't it odd?
You've a dime's worth of something known only to God!"

These are seeds, but the plants and the blossoms are here
With their petals of various hues;
In these little pellets, so dry and so queer,
There is power which no chemist can fuse.
Here is one of God's miracles soon to unfold,
Thus for ten cents an ounce is Divinity sold!

-Author unknown

Notes

Things I want to do, or remember from the last chapter:

....
....
....
....
....
....
....
....
....
....
....
....
....
....
....
....
....
....
....
....
....

Chapter 3

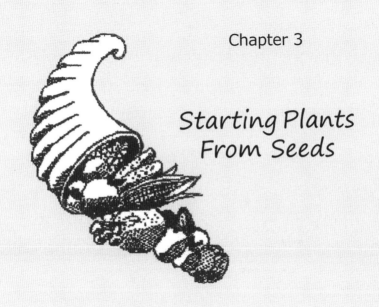

Starting Plants
From Seeds

Starting Plants From Seed

Before we get into the nitty-gritty of this topic, here's a little tip on growing stronger, healthier plants from seed: I remember Grandma gently running her hand back and forth, over the tops of her tomato plants, after they were about 2" tall. Folks back in those days called this 'massaging the sprouts', and this hand gesture was necessary if the farm didn't have electricity.

What this does, is to help the seedlings build strong stems as well as to provide a fresh supply of carbon dioxide to the plants. Nowadays, you can easily accomplish this trick by setting up a small fan to blow a gentle breeze over the little buggers, being careful not to dry out the growing medium in the process. I have used a fan on my own tomato pants, and it really works!

When To Start The Seeds

Where we live, along the front range of the Rocky Mountains, most gardeners I know first set up their germination flats around February 15. My own experience is that this allows the tomato plants to grow to over 10" tall before setting them out sometime in late April, or early May. To protect them from frost, use 'Walls O' Water,' described further in this chapter.

Be Sure To Sanitize Everything

Make an honest effort to sanitize all of your seeding trays, tools, etc. before you begin. This is particularly

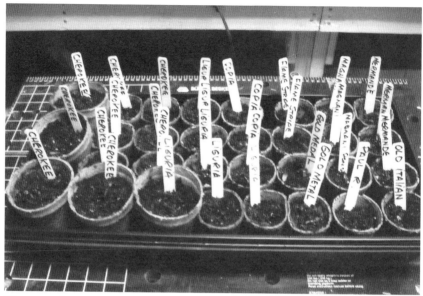
Tiny seeds sown in Winter will turn into the big dreams of Summer.

'Wall O' Water' might be your best friend to protect those tender plants from late frost or freeze. These worked for me even down to 25 degrees. Take care of them and they will last for years!

necessary if you decide to use the same equipment from last year. Sanitizing everything will prevent holdover pathogens and bacteria from invading your tender plants during their sprouting and early growth periods.

IMPORTANT! Do not use soil from the garden to fill the cells of your trays, as you will only succeed in dragging in all kinds of weed seed, insect eggs, fungus, etc. You get the point. Almost all commercial mixes are better to use and contain a good balance of peat, pumice, bark dust and vermiculite. You might want to avoid using the ones which contain time-released fertilizers in the blend. If you use the liquid plant energy formula we list toward the end of this chapter, you will be far better off, and it will be much cheaper than the material you buy in the store.

Which Kinds of Veggies Should I Start?

The best, and most popular one, is tomato, because you can start it much earlier than all the rest. If you count backwards two weeks from the normal last frost period for your location (your local extension agent will know) you should be able to start some of the **other** varieties, like squash, beets, kohlrabi, eggplant, melon, and pumpkins. All the rest will likely do better if planted directly into the soil, or purchased as starter plants from the nursery.

Where Can I Buy Heirloom Seed?

In addition to local nurseries, there is a list of reputable seed companies in Chapter 17.

What Kind Of Lights Do I need?

Take a common florescent 'shop light' fixture and replace the bulbs with two grow lights of the same length. These are called WIDE-SPECTRUM 40-watt bulbs and are available at good hardware and home-supply stores everywhere. Once you have sown your seeds, place these lights about 2-4 inches above the trays and leave them on for 24 hours until the seedlings have sprouted, and are about 2 inches high. I usually use my furnace room as my 'germination chamber' as it offers just enough heat and is out of the way from other activities.

Use Tea Water to Germinate Seeds

One of the oldest tricks in the book when it comes to germinating seeds is to use 'tea water'. Make it by putting two regular tea bags (black or green) in a one-gallon jug. Apply as a soak in the very beginning, and then only when the potting medium dries out. It is said that the tanic acid in tea helps to break down the seed coat resulting in faster germination. This would apply particularly for plants that have large or hard seeds.

After plants are about 2 inches tall, adjust the lights (and keep adjusting as they grow) so the lights are about 2 inches above the top of the plants. From this point on, leave the lights on for 12-16 hours a day. By turning them off for several hours a day, this will give the seedlings a chance to rest, and they won't get too 'leggy'. Turn the fan off during this resting period as well.

Hardening Off Your Seedlings

The process of acclimating seedlings to life outside of the indoor 'nursery' is called hardening off. You should start this about 2-3 weeks before transplanting in the garden. Set the flats, or pots, outside in a shady spot, and keep them from drying out during the day. Start by leaving them out for no more than 4-6 hours, then gradually increase exposure to all day. It's also OK to move them gradually into more full sun exposure, but you can easily burn the tender leaves with too much sun.

Of course you should keep an eye on the sky and bring all plants back indoors during inclement weather. All during this time of growing out your prized young seedlings, you should use a good starter fertilizer. There are many good formulations, but few better than the following one. You can blend it with ease, and use it during all of the seedling-to-transplant phase. Don't use straight water, and use this every time the soil is dry:

(Makes one gallon of fertilizer)

1 tablespoon of fish emulsion
1/2 tablespoon of Miracle Grow Tomato Fertilizer
1/4 teaspoon of epsom salts
3 tablespoons Coke soda pop

Once the transplanted tomatoes are firmly established, you should let the soil provide the natural fertilizer and humic acids to feed the plants. If you decide to use the 'dairy compost tea' soaked in corn cobs (see Chapter 6) you will even have nature's own time-release fertilizer to feed your plants.

Protect Plants From Frost

One of the luxuries of modern-day gardening comes in the form of a product known as Walls O' Water. Grandma used hot caps, which are little more than thick paper surrounding a wire frame. But Walls O' Water (see photo) are water-filled tubes which draw heat during the day, then dispense it to the plants at night. In addition, they protect young plants from wind damage, and even add structure to support the plants as they grow to 16" or more in height. When the tomato plants reach this height, it's time to take them off and store until next season. If you're careful not to poke a hole in them, they will last several years. Mine are going on five seasons.

One Final Point About Heirlooms

When you start your own plants from seed you have purchased from a reputable seed house, you are more than likely to get the true variety, not a hybrid from a hothouse grower. The last two seasons, I had a little extra space left over in the tomato patch, so I bought two heirloom tomato plants from a local home-supply store. They turned out to be sort of a rogue variety, still an heirloom, but not exactly what I was expecting. Nurseries are your next best bet, if you don't grow your own. This is where the real pro's work and they are almost always on hand to help you.

"One of the most delightful things about a garden is the anticipation it provides."
--W.E. Johns

"Earth is here so kind, that just tickle her with a hoe and she laughs with a harvest"
--Douglas Williams Jerrold

"The best fertilizer is the gardener's shadow."
--Author Unknown

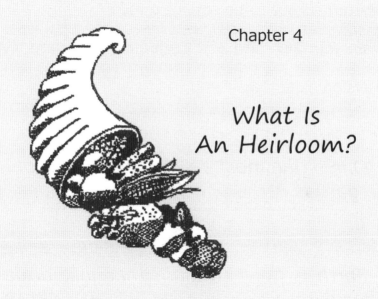

Chapter 4

What Is
An Heirloom?

Where Did I Buy The Best Seed Last Year?

_____

_____

_____

_____

_____

_____

Plants?

_____

_____

_____

What Is An Heirloom And Why Are They Popular?

(Most Of Grandma's Veggies Were Heirlooms)

An heirloom vegetable is a non-hybrid, open-pollinated variety which has been passed down from generation to generation. These species may be extremely rare, and in some cases, can be traced back hundreds of years to their origins on any of the seven continents.

Heirlooms are fast becoming the darlings of the seed industry and backyard gardeners. Their popularity is increasing as more and more types of vegetables called genetically modified organisms are introduced into the marketplace.

Many folks are leary of GMO's in the food chain, most often because they lack what is called 'lock-down proof' of their performance and safety. In addition, some incorporate a "terminator" gene that switches off the ability of the plant to produce viable seed. So you have to go back every year and buy more hybrid seed. Pretty clever, heh? You can't save it from one year to the next, because the seed is virtually dead. Even if you could, hybrids (not all are GMO's) rarely resemble their parents, often reverting to funky inbreds and throwbacks to strange ancestors.

For more information on GMO's, please see the next chapter, "Just What Are GMO's?"

Many heirloom tomato plants will eventually reach heights of 5 to 7 feet, and bear fruit right up to frost. This type of plant is an 'indeterminate.' Grand daughters like Taylor are always a big help!

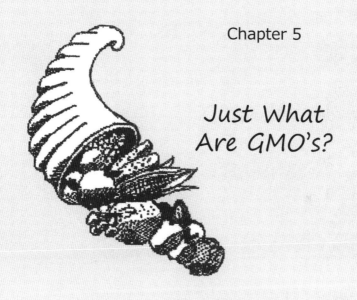

Chapter 5

*Just What
Are GMO's?*

Just What Are GMO's?

(Genetically Modified Organisms)

I think it was about the time they wanted to put mouse genes in my tomatoes (remember they said it would lengthen the shelf-life of the tomato?) that I said to myself, "I don't think I can take this 'modern' science anymore." And as if this weren't enough, they said 'well how about if we put fish genes in your strawberries, so they will stay nice and red longer?' I don't believe either of these controversial ideas ever made it past the news release of the genetic engineers responsible for their introduction. These new varieties were identified as genetically modified organisms.

Common Sense Trumps High IQ

What they DID accomplish however, was to make us think hard about what my wise father said to us kids some 50 or 60 years ago: "Intelligence is a wonderful thing, but it's a poor substitute for common sense."

I also like what Andy Rooney of CBS Television said not long ago about GMO's: "The federal government has sponsored research that has produced a tomato which is perfect in every respect, except you can't eat it. We should make every effort to make sure this disease, often referred to as 'progress', doesn't spread."

> *"All my hurts, my garden spade can heal."*
> --Ralph Waldo Emerson

The Call Of Spring

Behold the seeds

Waiting in the dark and cold

Winter soil

For the call of Spring.

Chapter 6

How To
Grow 'Killer'
Tomatoes

I have been thinking about the change of seasons. I don't want to miss Spring this year. I want to be there on the spot the moment the grass turns green.

.................Pilgrim at Tinker Creek

How to Grow 'Killer' Tomatoes

Is there anything on the face of the earth that tastes better than a red, ripe, juicy tomato, sprinkled with a little salt? Tomatoes are said to be the most widely-grown of all vegetables and as time goes on, more and more heirloom varieties are making their way into seed racks and catalogues all across America.

Tomatoes are not difficult to grow, given fertile soil, full sun, and adequate moisture. With this in mind, here is perhaps the best-kept secret from Grandma's garden for growing tantalizing tomatoes:

The Old Corncob Trick

Start by digging a hole where you wish to plant a tomato, about 12" wide and 16" deep. Next, take a 5-gallon bucket and dump 14-20 dry corncobs into the bucket. Then put two spadefuls of dry aged 100% dairy manure into the bucket, and fill the bucket with water. Drop two tablespoons of epsom salts in, a little humic acid if available, and stir it up vigorously for one full minute. Now you can dump everything into the hole, and top it all off with good black dirt.

Give this about an hour to 'set' (just about enough time to dig the rest of the holes you need), then transplant an heirloom tomato into its new home. The mixture that is poured into the hole was called by the old-timers "manure tea" and thousands of farmers and gardeners still testify as to its effectiveness. In my own garden, I have seen tomato plants grow to over seven feet high when fed this concoction. During the regular growing season, you should apply the liquid part of this blend once more, waiting until half-way through the summer for the second application.

What's with the epsom salt and corncobs? The epsom salts will help to prevent 'blossom-end rot', which is normally the result of calcium deficiency in the soil. The corncobs act as a natural time-release fertilizer, because they will soak up the manure tea, then dispense it slowly back into the soil, feeding the roots.

Use Round Wire Cages For Support

As your tomato vines grow (heirlooms are normally indeterminate in nature), they will need something to support them. I tend to shy away from the tomato towers as they are called, because the plants will easily outgrow the towers in a month or two. The best thing for my money is wire fencing material with openings about 4 by 6 inches wide. Make this into a round cage 16" wide and 4-6 feet high, and stake it with 2 by 2 inch wood poles pounded down into the dirt for a good 12 inches or more. Make sure the metal fencing is touching the ground to ensure natural air-borne electricity will infuse into the surrounding soil and help to stimulate plant growth. This wire fencing is sometimes called 'hog wire' and can be purchased at ranch & home stores.

Heirlooms Grow Longer Than Determinates

Vine is the correct term for heirloom varieties, as most are indeterminates, meaning they will continue to grow and produce fruit far beyond the ability of common determinates. The latter are more of a bush type, and produce fruit for a much shorter period of time, and then die off. Listed below are my favorite varieties which I have grown for several years: (See Chapter 17 for list of heirloom seed companies):

Name of Variety	Characteristics
Cherokee Purple	Medium size, purple when ripe, pink/green shoulders. Best tasting tomato of all types!
Homestead	Large size, turns light red when ripe. One of the oldest heirlooms around.
Mister Stripey	Striped yellow/red, can attain huge size. Low acid type, tends to be sweeter.
Beefsteak	World-famous large type, firm with great tomato taste and canning quality.
Black Krim	Luscious, heavy producer from Russia. Reddish-purple color when ripe. Medium size.
Roma	The traditional sauce and ketchup tomato. Shaped like a pear with few seeds.
Yellow Stuffer	Large fruit resembles bell pepper. Vines will produce up until very hard frost.
Red Cherry	Heavy producer of small, juicy salad types. Tempting just to snitch in garden!

Step 1 (left)--in making 'dairy compost tea': fill half a bucket with corncobs.

Step 2 (right)--place aged dairy compost in bucket with 2 tablespoons of epsom salts.

Step 3--fill bucket with water and mix well. Let stand for a couple of days, then dump into hole for tomatoes. They should look like this (left, above) in short time.

Finally, the heirloom 'maters you grow can produce some gigantic fruit. This one, right, is called 'Mr. Stripey.'

Chapter 7

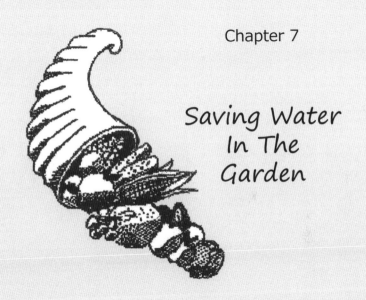

Saving Water
In The
Garden

How To Save Water In The Garden

Few topics have attracted as much attention recently as saving water and growing crops that use less of it. But with a little planning, and a few tricks, you can grow whatever you want, and your water bill won't bring you to your knees.

Grandma and Papa used a unique drip bottle method on all their vine crops like melons, cukes, squash, and pumpkins. This just might be THE most efficient way to water these vegetables, by providing a constant source of water in just the right amount, even if the soil only inches away stays hot and dry.

Bottle, Cork And Tube Trick

The bottle with a slow-drip tube inserted in the cork is the answer. (Look at the photo with this chapter to see how it's done.) By filling the container with water, and turning it upside down, the tube in the cork will allow only a drop or two to fall at one time. But that will keep the roots of the plant just moist enough to keep the plants growing in spite of any drought conditions around them. This is also a very good way to keep weeds at bay, as without moisture in the rows between the plants they won't grow nearly as fast, or spread.

Make sure you drill a hole in the cork the same size as the tube to enable the tube to slip through. I have used swizzlesticks on occasion that have just the right sized hole to let the water drip, not run. Once you get this far, the most challenging part of this might be how to hang the water bottle. I use three strong sticks bound together at the top (see attached photo), then I spread the sticks apart to form a triangle. Then I cut a pantleg from an old pair of jeans that is slightly smaller than the jug, but longer, then slip it over the bottle to hold it, and tie the long end to the top of the tripod. Use a rope about 8-10 inches long to do this. In this way, you can easily untie the bottle and remove the cork to refill it. One other advantage about the pantleg, is that it will absorb any moisture from around the bottle and keep the water inside from getting too warm.

Controlling The Amount Of 'Drip'

You can control the amount of water dripping from the bottle by inserting a smaller, or larger, tube through the cork. I have found that a one-gallon bottle will drip water for about two days. This will produce just enough water to keep the plant's roots moist. It works! For the 'mongo' size jug, I still remember how the old-timers would use a five-gallon jug, then leave their water wizards to take care of the vine crops for days on end. If that wasn't good old American entrepreneurism, I'll eat my hat!

If hanging the bottle seems too much work, you might get by with just laying the bottle down on the ground right next to the plant, tilting it slightly, and letting it drip out at will.

You should still cover the bottle with a light-colored pantleg to keep the water inside from getting too warm in the summer sun.

Here's Another Popular Option

To irrigate plants which are seeded in a continuous

row, as opposed to vine plants which are grown in mounds spaced several feet apart, use a soaker hose. Lay it upside down in the row, but be careful not to turn up the pressure too high, otherwise you will disturb the young seedlings and end up with a swamp on your hands. The same thing goes for the drip emitters mentioned above. In any event, try to avoid using an overhead sprinkler in the garden. This is a waste of water!!

Meet the most water-efficient device ever--the simple 'bottle dripper'.

Notes

Things I want to do, or remember from the last chapter:

....
....
....
....
....
....
....
....
....
....
....
....
....
....
....
....
....
....
....
....

Chapter 8

Planting
Back-To-Back
Crops

Planting Back-To-Back Crops

So you've sown your garden seeds, watered them diligently, hoed the pesky weeds, and done almost everything under the sun to make sure you produce a garden full of great vegetables. By now, (early summer), you've no doubt already eaten some of them, and are proud that all the hard work is beginning to pay off.

What do you do now? This is one of the easiest parts of gardening, yet one that will 'keep you in the green' for weeks to come. It's called back-to-back planting, or successive planting, and it's been done for ages. I remember that Grandma had a summer-long crop of the same varieties, and this is how she did it:

Rake The Soil Smooth

All you do is take a small rake and smooth over the bare soil in a row where you have already picked, or dug the first crop. Let's say it's beets we're talking here. Some of them will mature earlier than others, and these are the ones you will pluck as the first crop, leaving other small ones to mature. It's in this empty space you will smooth over and sow a second crop of beets. Just make sure you don't wash away those seeds when you irrigate during the warmer summer months ahead. This is where the beauty of the drip system, or soaker hose irrigation comes into play. You water only the seeds and soil in the row, not the tops of the plants or in between the rows where the wild west of weeds sets up camp.

By the way, whenever possible, avoid watering with an overhead sprinkler. It wastes water and money, and just as important, many plants are just like your average young boys; they frankly don't like to take showers (except for plants, thunderstorms are the real kind of shower which contain life-giving nitrogen, phosphorus and other critical elements).

A quick reminder here that when you harvest the very first crops of the season, don't throw away those tender tops. Many are good to eat. Those you choose not to consume, either lay down in the aisle between the rows to decompose, or put into the compost bin. This way you will be helping to produce more humus to add to your garden at the end of the growing season. Some of the varieties which folks save for their tops, or leaves, are beet, kohlrabi, turnip, and swiss chard. These can be steamed with thinly-sliced ham or beet, then served with butter and a little vinegar. I believe the word is SCRUMPTEELICIOUS. Of course the leafy crops like lettuce, endive, and spinach have already been picked in your garden for their tops.

Buy Enough Seed

Which varieties can you reseed as a second crop? Beans, beets, peppers, lettuce, spinach, endive and many of the popular herbs are all good candidates. Be sure to buy enough seed when you put in your first order for the second planting as well, as some seed houses and garden centers sometimes sell out of the more popular varieties later in the season.

If you have seed left over from one season to another, not to worry. Seed viability is usually pretty good at least until the next season. Be sure to store in a cool, dry place, and use a paper bag. I like to staple mine about head-high on the wall in my wood shop, away from mice and insects. For an excellent guide on how to save your own seeds from the best-performing varieties in your garden go to the website of Bounty Beyond Belief, a company listed at the back of this book under 'Heirloom Seed Companies'. Remember not to mess with saving seed from hybrids-- they usually don't come back to resemble their parents.

"An addiction to gardening is not all bad when you consider all the other choices in life."

--Cora Lee Bell

"If you've never experienced the joy of accomplishing more than you can imagine, plant a garden."

--Robert Brault

"The kiss of the sun for pardon, the song of the birds for mirth; One is nearer God's heart in a garden, than anywhere else on earth."

--Dorothy Frances Gurney

Notes

Things I want to do, or remember from the last chapter:

....
....
....
....
....
....
....
....
....
....
....
....
....
....
....
....
....
....
....
....

Chapter 9

Grandma's Top 10 Vegetables

Grandma's List of Her Top 10 Vegetables

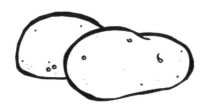

If you ever had the opportunity to taste ANYTHING that came out of Grandma's garden, you would have a hard time saying that any one vegetable was better than the another. But as far as utility (meaning it could be used in more ways than one) and taste was concerned, here's the way I believe Grannie would rate them:

1.--**Tomato**. Out-of-hand, table slicers, in BLT's, in soups and salads, as salsa, canned, and just simply made into tomato juice, this one clearly belongs at the top.

2.--**Potato**. One of the world's most popular staples in the garden. Eaten early as small 'new' potatoes, or left to mature, spuds will go a long way to serve a family well into the winter months.

3.--**Sweet Corn**. Another of the more popular staple veggies. If you can tie your coon dog up in the patch, you can produce a yummy crop of the world's most widely-planted vegetable. Freeze it, dry it, or eat it right on the cob--it's sheer delight!

4.--**Broccoli**. This is one plant that never gives up in producing bunch after bunch of crispy heads, even when you nip off the half-dollar size tops. It will even thrive into the second or third light frost of Autumn. Said to help immune system build defense against cancer.

5.--**Green Beans**. Cooked with a slice of bacon and some onion or garlic, can't you just smell them now, simmering on the kitchen stove! Yes, you can buy stringless heirlooms, like Grandma's.

6.--**Cucumbers**. Either sliced and served with a little vinegar, or packed into dill pickles, cukes are always a big item in any garden. To save space, grow them vertically on wire fencing material.

7.--**Onions & Garlic**. Two of the most versatile in your garden. There are dozens of ways to prepare them, and the medical world now says they help to lower the risk of cancer.

8.--**Carrots**. In soups, salads, in a roast or just eating out-of-hand, carrots are delicious fare. They will even over-winter in the soil with a layer of mulch around the crowns to prevent hard freezing.

9.--**Beets**. Can't beat the beet. They pickled a lot of beets back when I grew up and it seemed like my grandparents always served them at the dinner table. Also, fresh from the garden, they are normally simmered and served with butter and garlic salt.

10.--**Kohlrabi**. If you have ever been tempted to try it, and like the taste of cabbage or turnip, you might be in for a real treat. Slip a small chunk of ham into the steaming pot for extra flavor, or slice it raw into a green salad. A light frost in your garden improves the flavor, too, when eaten either raw, or cooked.

Here are some other varieties that might even make it into your own 'top ten': Cabbage, squash, turnip, peppers, pumpkin, radish, melon, eggplant, brussels sprouts, peas, asparagus, and perhaps many herbs.

A good back-saving way to plant potatoes--sharpen a 2x2 and poke a hole about 6" deep in the ridged-up row. Holes can be as close as 8" apart.

Final step is to let the little guys stick the spud sets in the hole and cover. Michael (and his brother Jakob, photo inset) both started helping in the garden at 4 years old.

Notes

Things I want to do, or remember from the last chapter:

....
....
....
....
....
....
....
....
....
....
....
....
....
....
....
....
....
....
....
....
....

Chapter 10

HOORAY!
It's Harvest
Time!

HOORAY! It's Harvest Time

Wait! Before you pick up that weathered reed basket and head out to harvest the first fruits of your little patch of paradise, you owe yourself a little reward. So grab a bottle of your favorite beverage, (perhaps wine if you're old enough to sip), and plop down on the bench overlooking the garden. As you enjoy the taste of someone else's labor, reflect for a moment on your own accomplishments and what it means to you. I like what John Ruskin once said: *"The highest reward for man's toil is not what he gets for it, but what he becomes of it."*

That's pretty deep philosophy for what many consider just a hobby, but gardening has a way of bringing out the best in everyone.

Remember To Share

One more thing before you get up from that bench to collect your just rewards. Don't forget the needy in your town who might be down on their luck or unable to grow a garden. Chapter 14 in this book implores those of us fortunate enough to have sufficient food stocks to not forget our neighbors and friends.

The reward of harvesting those delicious vegetables at their prime is both a sensual and mental experience. When all that hard work and worry over your 'summer love' proves out, and your heart feels light, it's almost like a kiss in the candy store from a pretty girl!

Ok, now you can go for it! I hope you have remembered to bring a salt shaker with you as you walked to the garden. As we mused earlier, is there anything on the face of the earth that tastes better than a big, juicy, ripe tomato with a little salt sprinkled on it!

Canned peaches, pickles, and salsa--just rewards for all that hard work!

There's some mighty fine eatin' in this pile of six varieties of squash.

Chapter 11

Grandma's Favorite Recipes

Grandma's Favorite Recipes

Remember going to Grandma and Grandpa's house and the mouth-watering aroma of Grandma's cooking that greeted you as soon as you stepped into the house? Or how about that scrumptious chocolate cake she would bring to your house for special occasions?

On the following pages, you'll find six old-fashioned recipes that will take you back to those days. For even more recipes, look for our next book "*Secrets From Grandma's Kitchen*" which will be released early Summer 2011.

Homemade Chicken & Noodles

1 2-3 lb. Chicken	*1 garlic clove*
1 quart chicken broth	*1 teaspoon salt*
1 quart water	*1 teaspoon pepper*

How to make the noodles: beat together one egg, one tsp olive oil, 1/2 tsp salt, 1/2 tsp pepper, 1/2 tsp dill weed, two tbsp warm butter, and one cup whole milk. Add just enough flour to make a non-sticky dough ball.

First of all, roll the dough ball for noodles onto a floured surface and cut into thin strips. Set aside to dry for 30-40 minutes.

In a deep pot, cover a whole 2-3 lb. chicken with a

quart of chicken broth, the water, the garlic clove, salt and pepper, and bring to a boil. Turn down heat and simmer with the lid on for 30 minutes. Take chicken out and debone it, also discarding the skin and some of the fat. Next, add back the noodles into the broth and cook for another 30 minutes on low heat with the lid covering only 2/3 of the pot.

Grandma's Deep Dish Apple Pie

Apple pie might just be Americas favorite dessert. We're going to enhance the flavor of this recipe by adding a few raisins!

8 large tart apples	*1/2 teaspoon nutmeg*
1 cup sugar	*1/2 cup honey*
1/4 teaspoon salt	*2 tablespoons flour*
1 teaspoon cinnamon	*2 tablespoon of either*
1/4 teaspoon vanilla	*butter or margarine*
2 tablespoons apple cider	*1/2 cup raisins*

For pastry, use own favorite recipe. Use glass dish, pre-bake pastry at 350 degrees for 10 min.

Peel, core, and slice apples. Combine flour, cider, raisins, sugar, honey, salt, butter, vanilla and spices and mix into apples. Pour into 10" deep glass dish lined with pastry. Take strips of pastry and make horizontal rows across the top of pie 1" apart. Bake in preheated oven at 350 degrees for one hour.

This is a great recipe if the cook in the house has trouble getting the gardener(s) in for dinner on time. Just open the door, and the smell will have them running for the kitchen in record time!

Scalloped Fresh Sweet Corn

Once you've eaten your fill of corn-on-the cob (is that possible?), here's a great dish featuring that same fresh taste, but with a little twist:

4 tablespoons flour
1 teaspoon sea salt
1/2 teaspoon mustard
1 large egg
2 tablespoons butter
1 tablespoon Worcestershire sauce

4 tablespoons butter
1/2 cup chicken broth
1 quart sweet corn
1 cup cracker crumbs
1 cup milk

Blend Worcestershire sauce, flour, mustard, and salt with the butter in heavy saucepan. Add broth and milk gradually, and cook, stirring constantly, until thickened. Stir egg into corn and blend with sauce. Turn mixture into casserole dish and top with 2 tablespoons melted butter. Bake at 350 degrees until top is browned. Sprinkle with 1/4 cup of grated cheese. Wait 5 minutes to serve.

French Onion Soup

2 cups yellow onions, sliced
2 tablespoons butter
2 cups chicken broth
1 quart beef broth
1/2 teaspoon salt

1/4 teaspoon pepper
1/2 cup grated
cheddar cheese
4 slices french bread

Saute onions in butter for 10 minutes. Stir in broth, salt and pepper. Let simmer for 45 minutes. Pour into large soup bowls. Place bread slices over top of soup and sprinkle grated cheese over top of bread. Place bowls under broiler briefly to melt cheese. Serves 6.

Old-Fashioned Pot Roast

Beef rump or round,
3-4 pounds
1 teaspoon dill weed
1 tablespoon garlic salt
1 tablespoon pepper

1 tablespoon olive oil
1 onion, sliced
2 cups tomato juice
1/4 cup flour
6 bay leaves

Rub meat with olive oil. Combine flour with dill, salt, and pepper. Rub over meat. Slice onion and place around meat in roaster, or dutch oven. Pour tomato juice in pot. Place bay leaves on top of roast. May also put carrots and potatoes around edges of meat for complete meal. Cook at 350 degrees for two hours with lid on pot. To finish, take lid off and cook uncovered for one half hour at 300 degrees. Make gravy with brownings, one tsp of corn starch, 2 cups beef broth and salt to taste.

Aunt Effie's Old-Fashioned Dill Pickles

1 one-quart jar
1 garlic clove
6-7 small cucumbers

1/4 teaspoon alum powder
1 large dill floweret
Brine (see below)

--Follow below directions for each quart jar--

Sterilize 6-8 jars and lids in dishwasher. Pack jars with dill, alum, garlic, and cukes. To make brine, use enough of the following recipe for 2-1/2 cups in each jar: 2 cups cider vinegar, 6 cups water, 3/4 cup pickling salt. Bring the brine to a boil and cover cukes to within 1/4 inch of top.

Place in hot water bath on stove so water covers jar to within 2 inches of top. Place lid on pot, boil until bubbles start to come to top from inside the liquid of each jar. Seal with lids and store in a cool place. Good to eat in about a month, but longer enhances flavor. This recipe is well over 100 years old and a family favorite!

The recipes in this book, and the ones to come in the next, *Secrets From My Grandma's Kitchen*, have come down through the generations, and many are what you would call 'comfort foods'.

In reality, some are even more than that. They were, and still are, extraordinary health foods because of their claim to aid in either preventing, or mitigating effects of several diseases, or ailments.

Heirloom tomatoes, like this Beefsteak variety, are full of lycopene.

"I have never had so many good ideas day after day as when I worked in the garden."

--John Erskine

"There is no gardening without humility. Nature is constantly sending even its oldest scholars to the bottom of the class for some egregious blunder."

--Alfred Austin

Notes

Things I want to do, or remember from the last chapter:

....

....

....

....

....

....

....

....

....

....

....

....

....

....

....

....

....

....

....

....

Chapter 12

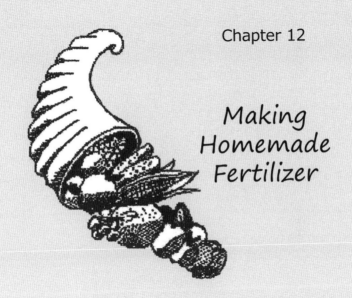

Making
Homemade
Fertilizer

How To Make Homemade Fertilizer

We know that humic acid is the best natural soil conditioner there is, but it takes time to develop in your compost pile, or garden. With that in mind, here are some good formulations you can brew up as 'tonics' in the meantime. Each has a different purpose and composition.

Remember to use gloves if you work with any fertilizer made from animal manure, as it might contain elements of e-coli. Good hygiene is always called for when you come in contact with soil, regardless of what miracles it might perform on plants:

A Good Spring Tonic

Right after you rotortill, or spade up your garden in very early Spring, is a good time to apply this blend over the plot to kick-start the microbial activity. The mix below will cover about 100 square feet:

1 cup liquid dish soap	2 cans of Coke
1 cup instant tea powder	1 can of beer
1 cup plain mouthwash	1 cup tobacco juice

Make the tobacco juice by emptying a can of smoking tobacco (strand type works best) into a quart of warm water. Let it seep for a day or two, then pour off liquid. What you don't use of this, you can save and blend into the last formulation in this chapter, *"An Effective Natural Pesticide."*

All-Purpose Natural Fertilizer

This is one of the best, and easiest to make of all the homemade fertilizers. It contains many of the trace elements necessary to build good soil. It might be a tad expensive to spread over the entire garden, so use it in close quarters around the crown of each plant, or mix into the compost pile.

1 cup fish emulsion　　*1 cup 'compost tea'**
1 cup dried seaweed　　*1/2 cup sugar*
1/4 cup epsom salts　　*1/2 cup coffee grounds*
1 quart water　　　　　*1 cup cottonseed meal*

* Dairy 'compost tea' described in Chapter 6.

Dilute this mixture 1 part above, to 1 part water. Use around immediate area of plants after growth exceeds 3-4 inches. Keep in a cool place.

An Effective Natural Pesticide

No harsh chemicals here! Bugs hate the taste of tobacco juice and garlic, and would make poor fans of Mexican food (hot peppers). Bad bugs also get their mouths washed out with soap and mouthwash.

1 cup liquid dish soap　　*1/2 cup hot peppers, cut*
1 cup plain mouthwash　　*2 quarts water*
1 cup tobacco juice　　　*3 cloves garlic, mashed*

Mix well and put aside for two days in a cool place. Strain bulk residue and dilute liquid 1:1 with water. Spray over vegetables at first sign of insect invasion. Avoid application in extreme heat of day. Tobacco juice formula found in *"A Good Spring Tonic"* blend listed earlier in this chapter.

One More Option

Here's one more formula for improving and conditioning poor soil. It does take time to work, so don't expect to plant into it for a good month or more. Make sure to dig it in so it can work with the natural microbes present to break up the hard ground and make it 'mellow'.

This will cover an area 10' by 10':

2 cups bone meal   *2 cups greensand*
6 cups cottonseed meal   *2 cups coffee grounds*
1 cup fish emulsion   *1 cup epsom salts*

Mix the bone meal, greensand, coffee grounds and cottonseed meal. Apply the dry ingredients over the ground, then mix fish emulsion and epsom salts in 1 quart of water and spread over the same 100 square feet. Water it in, but don't soak it. You might even want to cover it with plastic to keep the weeds in check while your plot breaks down.

Over 100 years old! Every gardener has a personal treasure and this is mine. This old hoe once belonged to Grandma Eversoll. It has five cutting edges: two sides, two corners and a blade. And made from the finest steel you could buy.

Notes

Things I want to do, or remember from the last chapter:

....
....
....
....
....
....
....
....
....
....
....
....
....
....
....
....
....
....
....

Chapter 13

Pass It On
To The
Grandkids

Others Who Might Like A Copy Of This Little Book:

_____

_____

_____

_____

_____

_____

_____

_____

_____

_____

Pass It On!

> "Why try to explain miracles to your kids, when you can just have them plant a garden."
>
> --*Robert Brault*

Most children are fascinated to watch tiny seeds sprout, continue to grow under their watchful eye, then produce something that is good to eat. And more than likely, they've already been introduced to growing seed at their school, as part of their required 'science project.' Teachers will tell you that sprouting seeds is among the most popular projects during elementary school studies.

Let Them Have Their Very Own!

So what's the key to keeping those impatient, short-attention-span youngsters interested in gardening? The most important thing might be to help them make a small plot 'their very own'. You probably don't want to make the mistake of saying "Do you want to help me with MINE"? Kids will develop a more keen sense of self-worth if they are allowed to take identity with their little patch of produce, even through the struggles and challenges sure to come.

Start out with something small, like one row of mixed vegetables of THEIR choice, and make sure you put a sign or label, at the end of the row that says 'Michael's, or Jakob's, or Taylor's, or Annie's, or Alex', etc. Help them plant it, teach them to care for it, and don't hover over them.

Try to make it as fun as possible. Their enthusiasm may wax and wane through the season, but if you keep the learning lesson short, their willingness to listen will be, like they say, right-on, dude.

Chris (daughter of the author), and her daughter, Taylor, are frequent visitors, and helpers, at Papa's 'garden beyond the gate'.

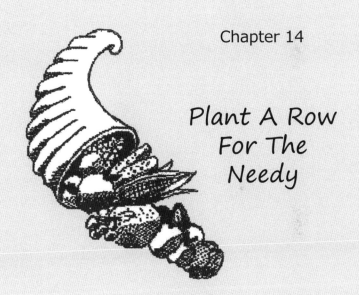

Chapter 14

Plant A Row
For The
Needy

Plant
A Row For
The Needy

Our country's pantries for the poor need your help, and fresh produce is one of the most appreciated of all contributions. Big hearts are happy hearts, and service above self can bring genuine satisfaction and humility to the giver.

Be sure to ask the young gardeners to help with this, as many of them have sincere empathy for others in need, especially around Thanksgiving.

Some companies will even provide seed for the purpose of growing food for those in need. Just ask your favorite local nursery.

"Give, and it will be given to you. Good measure, pressed down, shaken together, running over, all will be put into your lap." --Luke 6:38

"Let me be a little kinder, let me be a little blinder to the faults about me; let me praise a little more, let me be when I am weary, a little more cheery. Let me serve a little better, those I am striving for. Let me be a little braver, when temptation bids me waver. Let me strive a little harder to be all that I should be; let me be a little meeker to the brother that is weaker. Let me think more of my brother and a little less of me." --Anonymous

Notes

Things I want to do, or remember from the last chapter:

....
....
....
....
....
....
....
....
....
....
....
....
....
....
....
....
....
....
....
....
....
....

Chapter 15

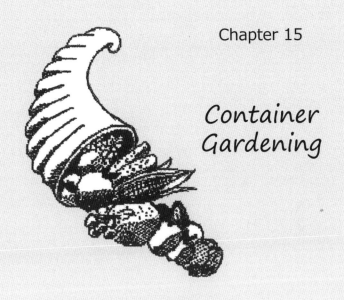

Container
Gardening

Container
Gardening

If you're just a beginning gardener, or don't have the space required for even a small garden, then container gardening is for you.

Container gardening can be economical, water-efficient, surprisingly productive, and a real space and time saver. I have even seen some remarkable 'garden' growing in pots on the balconies of high rise apartments, Where there's a will, there's often a way, and for city dwellers they're finding lots of ways to grow fresh, nutritious, homegrown vegetables in containers without a spade, rake, or hoe.

What kinds of vegetables can you grow in a container? And what kind of containers are suitable for a patio, windowsill, balcony, or even a narrow doorstep?

Anyone For A Salad?

Tomatoes, potatoes, peppers, carrots, beets, beans, green onion, lettuce, radish, spinach, and turnips are all suitable. You might not do so well with vining plants like cucumbers and squash unless you can provide them with a trellis or wire cage to accommodate their sprawling habit.

As far as the type of container goes, you can pretty well let your imagination run wild. Probably the most popular is the redwood type planter, although ceramic pots are a close second. Plastic pails, old bushel baskets, and even metal tubes have been used success-fully.

Good drainage is important in the container, and to achieve it, place 1" of gravel in the bottom. Then layer two pages of newspaper on top to prevent loss of soil. Make sure the container has a few holes in the bottom along the sides to avoid waterlogged soil and rotting roots.

Size Depends On Each Variety

The size of the container depends on the type of vegetable being planted, and space availability. Most herbs in addition to green onions, lettuce, radish and spinach will all do well in pots 6-10" in size. Two to three-gallon containers are better for carrots, beets, beans, kohlrabi, and turnips. Save the larger tubs (5-10 gallon) for tomatoes, potatoes, peppers, and rutabagas. These varieties all have deeper root systems and need the space.

If you decide to use clay pots, check often to make sure the potting soil doesn't dry out, as clay is porous and water will wick off faster than will wood or plastic containers.

Growing Media

Although soil mixes will hold water better than the synthetic mixes you can buy in practically any hardware or home supple store, the soil-less mixes (synthetic types) are better suited for container gardening for the reason they are free of disease and weed seeds.

They also drain well and are lightweight. They are mainly composed of peat moss, fine dirt, ground up tree bark, small amounts of sawdust, perlite or vermiculite. The more expensive types might also contain some type of time-release fertilizer, but if you mix up your own, you might not need to pay the extra money for a small amount of fertilizer. For several types of fertilizer you can make yourself, see Chapter 12, "Making Homemade Fertilizer".

Disease And Insects

The same diseases and insects that attack larger gardens can also invade container gardens. You should inspect your plants periodically for diseases and fruit-feeding insects. If you need to use a fungicide or insecticide, use only EPA-approved types, or contact your local county extension agent for the latest information on these subjects.

"The best things in life are nearest: breath in your nostrils, light in your eyes, flowers at your feet, duties at your hand, and the path of God before you."

--Robert Louis Stevenson

The Children's Garden at Spring Creek Gardens is famous for clever designs to engage youngsters in fun activities related to gardening.

Chapter 16

Little Known Facts

Little Known Facts About Vegetables

Did You Know? That potatoes and tomatoes are the most popular vegetables around the world! And strange as it may seem, they both belong to the nightshade family.

That dark green leafy vegetables (the darker, the better) have the most nutritional value. Some of these are broccoli, spinach, swiss chard, and romaine lettuce.

Carrots contain the anti-oxidant carotene and are an excellent source of vitamins B, C, and A (your body converts the carotene into A). It's a good idea to keep the skin on as it contains many of the vitamins and minerals.

Brussels sprouts are reputed to be cancer fighters, as they contain indole-3 carbinol, sulforaphane, and vitamins A and C. It's always better to steam them rather boil in water.

Garlic and its cousins, onion, leek, shalots, and chives are said by doctors to lower cholesterol and lower risk for stomach cancer. They are high in fiber and in some cases will help to stabilize blood pressure.

Cauliflower, like many fresh garden veggies, should be steamed, not boiled. They contain carbinol and bioflavonoids which have cancer fighting properties, plus have been shown to be good for the heart.

Beet greens actually have more nutrients in them than the roots. Used medicinally for centuries, beets contain betacyanin, an effective cancer-fighting agent. Betacyanin is also the pigment that gives beets their rich red color.

Eating sweet corn might make you smarter! That's because it contains high amounts of thiamine which is what the brain uses to produce acetylcholine, a neuro-transmitter.

Kohlrabi is actually a member of the cabbage family. Like many garden vegetables, it contains indoles, a chemical that reduces the effects of estrogen.

Peppers have been used for centuries to prevent infectious--particularly respiratory--illnesses. They contain capsaicin, which also reduces headaches.

Watermelons are not only delicious to eat, they also contain lycopene, an anti-oxidant known to reduce the risk of prostate cancer in men. It's also a source of vitamin B6 which helps to reduce stress. Maybe that's why you always see a big smile on the face of anyone eating watermelon.

Many a soul has passed through the garden gate to leave stress and strife behind and enter a sanctuary of relaxation and reward.

Chapter 17

*Heirloom
Seed
Companies*

Sources For Heirloom Seeds

(Editor's Note: Although there are virtually dozens of seed companies now offering heirloom varieties, the following six are known to have started from (and most still are) smaller family operations. They are recognized as having excellent reputations.)

Bounty Beyond Belief
6595 Odell Pl, #G
Boulder, CO 80301
(303) 530-1222
www.bbbseed.com

Heirloom Acres Seeds
2529 CR 338
New Bloomfield, MO 65063
(573) 491-3001
hierloomacresseeds.com

Seeds Trust
P.O. Box 596
Cornville, AZ 86325
(928) 649-3315
support3@seedtrust.com

Skyfire Garden Seeds
1313 23rd Road
Kanopolis, KS 67454
skyfiregardenseeds.com

Baker Creek Heirloom Seeds
2278 Baker Creek Road
Mansfield, MO 65702
(417) 924-8917
www.rareseeds.com

Victory Seed Company
P.O. Box 192
Molalla, OR 97038
(503) 829-3126
victoryseeds.com